Surfing in Color

Alyssa Mulligan

Copyright © 2021 ::: All Rights Reserved

Surfing in Color

COPYRIGHT © 2021 Alyssa Mulligan

ALL RIGHTS RESERVED

Photos by Alyssa Mulligan – Mullicaptures
Illustrations by Anat Sweeney
Editing by Charlotte Fletcher and Laila Kamarrudin
Front cover photo Mavericks in Half Moon Bay, photo by Alyssa Mulligan
Back cover photo Rodeo Beach, California, photo by Alyssa Mulligan

instagram.com/mullicaptures

EXCEPT FOR BRIEF EXCERPTS USED IN REVIEWS OR OTHER USES ALLOWED BY COPYRIGHT LAW, NO PART OF THIS BOOK MAY BE REPRODUCED OR TRANSMITTED IN ANY FORM OR ANY MANNER, ELECTRONIC OR MECHANICAL, INCLUDING PHOTOCOPYING OR RECORDING, OR BY ANY INFORMATION STORAGE AND RETRIEVAL SYSTEM, WITHOUT ADVANCE PERMISSION IN WRITING FROM THE AUTHOR.

ISBN-13: 978-0-578-90790-1

Color Palette

This color palette is an example for children or adults who enjoy expressing the emotions through coloring. The calming effect of matching one's feelings with colors helps instill a peaceful state of mind. Below are some examples of colors to match emotions:

red	strong	green	joyful
dark orange	amused	dark green	interested
light orange	proud	turquoise	powerful
yellow	happy	blue	peaceful
pale green	excited	purple	shy

Photo Pages:

INTRODUCTION 1
RODEO BEACH 2
PEBBLE BEACH 4
OCEAN BEACH, SAN FRANCISCO 6
SANTA MONICA PIER 8
RODEO BEACH 10
BIG SUR 12
OCEAN BEACH 14
RODEO BEACH 16
BIG SUR 18
MAVERICKS BEACH, HALF MOON BAY 20
TURKS AND CAICOS ISLANDS 22
GOLDEN GATE NATIONAL RECREATION AREA 24
BIG SUR 26
RODEO BEACH 28
RODEO BEACH 30
BIG SUR 32
STINSON BEACH, MARIN COUNTY 34
CAMPING AT BIG SUR 36
WAIKIKI, HAWAII 38
ABOUT THE PHOTOGRAPHER 40
SOURCES 43

Introduction

Surfing in Color features photographs by 17-year-old Alyssa Mulligan, a junior at Marin Catholic High School in Kentfield, California.

Alyssa was inspired to create this book by her appreciation of oceans and beaches in Northern California. She is the founder of Mullicaptures, a photography-based company. Her photos sell in pottery stores and at sporting events, and her work has been published in California venues and magazines.

For this project, Alyssa worked with illustrator Anat Kafry Sweeney to capture the raw essence and beauty she sees through the lens of her camera and translate it into a coloring book for children. Alyssa donates a share of her books to underprivileged children in hopes of bringing some of the beaches and oceans to life for them.

Follow Alyssa on her Instagram page at instagram.com/mullicaptures

Rodeo Beach

Rodeo is a wide sandy beach on the piece of land that separates Rodeo Lagoon from Rodeo Cove on the west side to the Marin Headlands in the Golden Gate National Recreational Area. In the winter and fall, it can have moderate short period waves from the northwest. The beach is nestled in the base of the Marin Headlands. Rodeo has light winds with clean conditions and is a popular surf break among Marin County and San Francisco residents.

Pebble Beach

Pebble Beach is home to the world-famous golf course, in between Monterey and Carmel-by-the-Sea, California. It has picturesque cliffs often covered with wildflowers including California poppy, sea kale, and ice plant.

Ocean Beach, San Francisco

Ocean Beach is one of the most well-known surfing beaches in the Bay Area. Ocean Beach was once separated from the rest of San Francisco by huge sand dunes, but these were developed in the past century so many buildings are now close to the ocean. Ocean Beach is a good site for experienced surfers with knowledge of the area, because it can have dangerous currents.

Santa Monica Pier

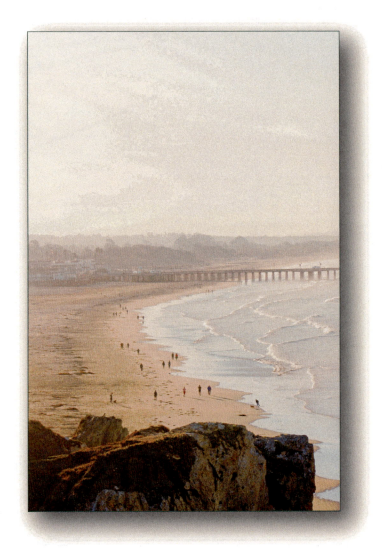

The Santa Monica Pier is in Los Angeles, California and is more than 100 years old. Built in 1909, the pier features concession stands, an amusement park, and incredible views of the beach and the ocean. The beach itself spans 3½ miles of beautiful white sand edging the warm ocean waters of Southern California.

Rodeo Beach

In the cliffs along Rodeo Beach, a World War II military post called Fort Cronkhite was built in 1941 to protect the San Francisco Bay Area. Local residents shortened Fort Cronkhite to "Cron," which is the common name used among surfers for this beach area.

Big Sur

Big Sur is a beautiful natural area along California's coastal Highway 1. The state park here offers camping, hiking, amazing redwood trees, and stunning beaches. The Big Sur River runs through the park and draws visitors to its crystal-clear waters all year round.

Ocean Beach

Ocean Beach is on the west coast of San Francisco, adjacent to Golden Gate Park and the Sunset District. The water here averages about 56 degrees, so you'll see surfers in wetsuits! In the winter, waves are often 12 feet or higher, and the cold temperatures can limit the crowd sizes.

Rodeo Beach

Rodeo Beach is a popular spot for tourists because of its Sausalito location. Beginning surfers can enjoy this beach area but should be careful of windy conditions and the rocky shore. It's just a couple miles north of the Golden Gate Bridge, located in the Golden Gate National Recreation Area.

Big Sur

Big Sur is a popular spot for surfers from all over Northern California; around 4.5 million tourists visit Big Sur every year. The name "Big Sur" comes from the Spanish "El Sur Grande," which means The Big South; settlers who arrived here in the late 1700s gave it this nickname. Big Sur is a rugged stretch of California's central coast situated between Carmel and San Simeon, with the Santa Lucia Mountains rising to the east.

Mavericks Beach, Half Moon Bay

Mavericks is one of the world's most well-known – and dangerous – surf areas on the West Coast. To get out to the massive waves, surfers often take boats or jet skis to get from the beach to where the waves break. International surf competitions are hosted here at Mavericks, with surfers traveling from around the world to enjoy this famous beach.

Turks and Caicos Islands

Turks and Caicos are a group of 40 islands in the Atlantic Ocean, known for their turquoise waters and white sand beaches. The coral islands are south of the Bahamas and are a British Overseas Territory.

Golden Gate National Recreation Area

In the Golden Gate NRA are more than 2,000 plant and animal species! This area features terrestrial, coastal, and marine environments, and it offers visitors more than 80,000 acres stretching across three counties.

Big Sur

Big Sur's 90 miles of beaches has been called the "longest and most scenic stretch of undeveloped coastline in the United States." Even though it is a beautiful park, Big Sur remains undeveloped and uncrowded by tourists, so it is the perfect place to visit if you want a relaxed day in nature.

Rodeo Beach

Rodeo Beach is just a few miles northwest of San Francisco's famous Golden Gate Bridge. The sand here is made up of small red and green pebbles and is edged on both sides by beautiful cliffs that can be hiked for amazing views of the San Francisco Bay.

Rodeo Beach

Rodeo is a beautiful pebbly beach popular with surfers. Down the hill from Battery Townsley, the beach is tucked between Fort Cronkhite and the Marin Headlands Visitor Center. The area features outdoor barbecue grills and picnic tables and is thus popular with families and groups.

Big Sur

The autumn months between September and November are the best times to surf the waves at Big Sur. During this season, the waves have the best shape and size for surfers of various skill levels, and the water is still relatively warm from the summer season. Sometimes you may have to hike with your board to reach the best surfing spots, but it will definitely be worth it when you get out on the water!

Stinson Beach, Marin County

People who live in Marin County often name Stinson as the area's most popular beach. In the summertime, the sunny days, white sand, and easy-to-reach location make Stinson Beach the destination of choice for many surfers and families. There are even some dog-friendly areas here, so you don't have to leave your pup at home!

Camping at Big Sur

Several campgrounds are available near the prettiest beaches at Big Sur. It's a very popular area, and reservations often are full six months in advance. Though state park campgrounds may be full, camping is allowed in many areas of the Los Padres National Forest or on Bureau of Land Management sites.

Waikiki, Hawaii

Honolulu is the capital of the Hawaiian Islands, and on its south shore is the world-famous neighborhood of Waikiki – once home to the royal Hawaiian family. Waikiki means "spouting waters." Along with its pristine beaches and beautiful resorts, Hawaii is home to an abundance of tropical birds and other wildlife, including many species of fish, dolphins, sea turtles, whales, and sharks.

About the Photographer

At the age of three, my bare feet were first exposed to the big, blue puddle called the ocean. It was from that moment that I began to grow a deep love for the frigid water as it washed up on my toes. My parents took me to the beach almost every weekend; I grew up near some of the most beautiful beaches in northern California, including Ocean Beach in San Francisco. My favorite part about our weekend escapades was arriving at the beach when that first view of the sand overwhelmed me; a feeling of tranquility and peace overloaded my senses. The beach thrilled, inspired, and always excited me, and I love the ocean's magnificence. I was enamored with the bright reflection of water from the horizon and how it refracted from the white sun's glare to glitter on the ocean's surface.

~ *Alyssa Shea Mulligan*

Why did you choose beaches for this book?
The beach has always been a memorable and cherished place for me. Here in California, there are so many different beaches, each with its own personality that makes it unique – and fun to photograph! As a child I often traveled to the beach with my parents and the salty air and foamy waves became a second home to me, as well as a place to explore. We made many beach excursions that contributed to my knowledge and sparked my interest in the beaches near the Bay Area in California. I started surfing in 5th grade when I went to a surf camp in Santa Cruz taught by national surfers, and since then I have fallen even more in love with the ocean.

What inspires you as you walk on a beach?
The beach is for me both a getaway and a chance to connect with nature. The mesmerizing sounds of the splashing waves inspire me to photograph the

serenity the beach offers to people who visit. I hope to share the beauty of the beach with those who may not be able to see it in person.

Do you use any special photography or lighting techniques?
I try to go at sunrise or sunset for my best images. This golden-hour light allows for warmer tones that are not so prevalent on the water and the beach. Sometimes on a windier day, I bring a tripod to balance and steady my camera; this allows me to get crisp shots without having to edit for blurriness in post-production.

What type of camera and lens do you use?
I shoot a Canon EOS T6. I switch off between different lenses, but usually I rely on a 75-200 lens to get clear zoomed-in shots – as well as a common 50-120 lens when shooting up close.

How long have you been taking pictures?
I have been shooting photos since the age of 11. I started taking photos of my friends for portraits; however, as I developed as a photographer, I found my target niche, which is nature and the ocean. I started taking professional photos at age 15 for magazines, events, blogs, and Instagram.

What do you love about surfing?
I love surfing because it is one of the most casual sports out there. Surfing is for everyone, and anyone can learn and be good at it. It just takes practice!

What do you hope kids appreciate from this coloring book?
Coloring can be a chance to relax and engage the mind; my hope is that it connects young people with ocean life, sea animals, the shoreline scenery, and the essence of surfing. I enjoyed coloring the most between the ages of 5 and 10. I think this age group is at their most creative and imaginative, and I hope to encourage children to be inspired as they approach these sketches.

Sources:

California State Parks, State of California. "PfeifferBig Sur SP." *CA State Parks*, www.parks.ca.gov/?page_id=570

"Fort Cronkhite." *National Park Service*, U.S. Department of the Interior, www.nps.gov/goga/learn/historyculture/fort-cronkhite.htm

"Fort Cronkite Rodeo Beach." *Surf Forecast Surf Report*, www.surf-forecast.com/breaks/Fort-Cronkite-Rodeo-Beach/forecasts/latest/six_day

"Golf Resorts, Courses & Spa Vacations." *Pebble Beach Resorts*, www.pebblebeach.com/

"Marin County Surf Report & Surf Forecast with LiveSurf Webcams - Magicseaweed." *Magicseaweed.com*, magicseaweed.com/Marin-County-Surf-Report/307/

"Ocean Beach." Golden Gate National Parks Conservancy, 15 May 2019, www.parksconservancy.org/parks/ocean-beach

"Rodeo Beach, Sausalito, CA." *California Beaches*, www.californiabeaches.com/beach/rodeo-beach/

"Rodeo Beach." Golden Gate National Parks Conservancy, 20 Dec. 2018, www.parksconservancy.org/parks/rodeo-beach

"Santa Monica Pier & Beach." *Visit California*, 5 Oct. 2019, www.visitcalifornia.com/uk/attraction/santa-monica-pier-beach

"Stinson Beach." *National Park Service*, U.S. Department of the Interior, www.nps.gov/goga/stbe.htm

"The Best Surf Spots in Big Sur." *Surfertoday*, www.surfertoday.com/surfing/the-best-surf-spots-in-big-sur

"Ventana Big Sur." Big Sur Natural History & Wildlife | Ventana Big Sur | Big Sur *Hotels*, www.ventanabigsur.com/big-sur/natural-history

"Waikiki." *Go Hawaii*, 29 May 2019, www.gohawaii.com/islands/oahu/regions/honolulu/Waikiki

Made in the USA
Las Vegas, NV
30 January 2022